UFOs

over Devon

Jonathan Downes

Bossiney Books · Launceston

for Maxine
with love

First published 2000 by Bossiney Books
Langore, Launceston, Cornwall PL15 8LD
Copyright © 2000 Jonathan Downes
All rights reserved
ISBN 1-899383-37-9
Cover illustration by Andrew Jago
Printed in Great Britain by R Booth (Troutbeck Press), Mabe, Cornwall

INTRODUCTION

In the summer of 1947, a pilot called Kenneth Arnold ushered in the modern UFO era. He was alone in a Callair aircraft, informally engaged on a search for a crashed C-46 marine transport plane near Mount Rainier in the Cascade Mountains of Washington State, USA, when he witnessed nine saucer-shaped objects in flight. He estimated their speed to be between 1300 and 1700 miles per hour, which would have been faster than any plane of the day could fly.

Although the sighting itself was of little significance, it attracted a hitherto unprecedented level of media interest, and kick-started a public fascination with unidentified flying objects which shows little sign of abating.

Fifty years after Arnold's experience, together with various members of the Exeter Strange Phenomena Research Group, I was lying on a heather-covered hillside at Woodbury Castle in East Devon. At about 11.00 pm all seven of us saw what seemed like a very dim blue-white star moving erratically just within the burgeoning cloud cover. We watched it for several minutes – the best visual analogy I can give is that it looked like a quasi-stellar version of the whirligig beetles which whizz around on the surface of ponds and slow-moving streams during hot summers.

Until then I hadn't really been interested in UFOs. I had always vaguely known that they existed, but it had not been a subject which had interested me. Those three minutes changed my life, and I became determined to find out as much as I could about the phenomenon.

Over the next few years I discovered that Devon had been a hotbed of UFO activity for decades, but as I avidly collected more and more data I discovered that, as Oscar Wilde once said, 'the truth is never pure and seldom simple'. Here, for the first time, I have gathered together some of the most intriguing UFO reports from the Devonshire skies during the last hundred years or so. The vast majority of these incidents took place in the vicinity of Woodbury Common in East Devon. This in itself might seem odd but, as I pointed out in my book *The Rising of the Moon – The Devonshire UFO Triangle* (1998), there is a long tradition of strangeness in that particular area – and UFOs are merely one part of the extraordinary range of bizarre occurrences which have been reported.

However, it would be silly to pretend that in Devon UFOs (whatever they actually are) are seen *only* near Woodbury Common, and in this book there are also accounts from Dartmoor, Tavistock and the South Hams. But one mystery has always confused and mildly puzzled me, and that is the paucity of reports from North Devon. Indeed in all the years I have been studying the subject I have come across no more than two North Devon UFO stories.

The first was from the summer of 1997, when two observers at Braunton saw what they described as 'a spherical bright yellow light flying inland from the Bristol Channel'. They watched it for several minutes before it disappeared.

The other account on file is rather more interesting. During autumn 1998 a vague acquaintance of mine was driving towards Barnstaple. She saw a white ball of light hovering above the dual carriageway, and reported to me later that she was sure beams of light were issuing from beneath an object towards the ground.

She told friends afterwards that she had experienced a 'feeling of euphoria' during the incident and also perhaps of missing time, but as she hadn't really been aware of the precise time she couldn't comment on this matter to any great degree.

Finally, although I have drawn certain conclusions from the data I have presented in *UFOs over Devon*, the most important thing that has come out of my researches is the certain knowledge that, not only is the universe an infinitely strange and wonderful place in which to live, but there are mysteries to be solved everywhere – even in the sleepy Devon countryside.

THE EARLY YEARS

The earliest Devonshire UFO sighting I have managed to uncover is from May 1909 when the *Exmouth Journal* recounted that:

'Exmouth was thrown into a state of amused excitement on Thursday by an allusion to the "flitting" about in the firmament of an airship with the accompanying fears of foreign invasion and its attendant horrors. Whatever was the "mysterious" affair which was noticed by two girls as long ago as last Friday night, it was only on Wednesday that it was "licked into airship shape" and remembering the elusive – may it be suggested the illusive [sic] – quality of the craft, it became quite natural to speculate as to its mission or presence. That it was only seen by two young girls – Miss Violet Woodcock, and Miss Cissie Webber – and had evaded the vigilance of the coastguard men, gave the story [a] mysterious complexion… Indeed, its ubiquitous quality surrounded it with quite an air of wonder.

'However, the story of two young ladies, who did not themselves proclaim that they had seen an airship is very simple, and can be explained in two ways. At the time – between nine thirty and ten p.m. – they were returning home by way of Alexandra Terrace, after a walk on the Esplanade. They noticed a light flash over the ground, and looking upward in the direction of the sea, they saw another flash or two. They appeared to be frightened a little, and went home, where they incidentally alluded to the matter. They had no idea themselves of airships at the time, nor had they imagined since that they had seen lights flashed from an airship, imaginary or real. What they saw is suggested to be what is popularly called "shooting stars" or possibly searchlights from vessels at sea. Very little notice was taken of the matter generally, as from the first it was regarded as an idle rumour.'

This was only one of many sightings of what became known

as 'mystery airships' which were watched across Britain, and indeed the world, that summer. They were seen in such diverse spots as Kazhakstan and Australia, as well as across North America, and it is interesting to note that wherever they were located witnesses ascribed them to secret military technology of an unfriendly power. So in central Asia they were identified as reconaissance balloons from British India, and in the UK and North America they were said to be mystery airships of the Kaiser! However, they were almost certainly nothing of the sort because, if they were indeed machines, the technology described was far beyond anything available to any military power on earth at the time.

The British Government were certainly concerned about these incidents. Admiralty documents recently discovered in the Public Records Office at Kew confirm rumours that the Royal Naval Intelligence Office at Plymouth had investigated a series of sightings of floating lights seen on Dartmoor during the summer of 1914.

On 28 June 1914 two naval officers interviewed Miss Cecilia Peel-Yates, of Ashburton. They described her as a 'well educated gentlewoman of considerable intelligence' who had travelled widely and 'talked with a knowledge of the world that entitled her statements to be received with respect'.

The investigating officers established that: 'a few mornings previously, just before dawn, having been awakened by the barking of dogs, she saw from her bedroom window a bright light in the sky bearing north, and apparently suspended a short distance above the earth'. She described it as being too large and bright to have been a planet, and 'as she watched, it swung away to the north-east and disappeared'.

This was far from being an isolated incident. A few weeks later Mrs Cave-Penny and her daughter, who lived near Hexworthy on Dartmoor, told the investigating team that 'on several occasions they had watched a bright white light rise from a point a

6

few hundred yards to the eastward' of a disused mine. Unfortunately for the present day chroniclers of the uncanny the Admiralty documents are no more helpful than that, and the precise location of the 'disused mine' has been lost in the sands of time.

Later that summer the same light was reported from two locations near Totnes, and similar phenomena were observed throughout the autumn. By this time Britain was firmly involved in a long and bloody war with Kaiser Wilhelm's Germany and it could well be seen as significant that the Admiralty nevertheless devoted so many man hours to investigating these phenomena.

No doubt there are further documents on these cases still hidden in official files at the Public Records Office, but they have not yet been released into the public domain and so nearly a century after the events I am unable to ascertain what, if any, conclusions the Admiralty drew at the time.

It is tempting to fantasise a scenario in which the conclusions were so terrifying that even now we are not allowed to be told the truth. However, it is more likely that, as with so many official investigations into unexplained phenomena, the enquiries merely fizzled out and the powers that be preferred to concentrate their efforts on the Great War, and the more tangible threat posed to the British Empire by the combined might of the German and Austro-Hungarian Empires!

THE ROSWELL ERA

It wasn't until after the Second World War that the modern age of UFOlogy started in earnest. The Kenneth Arnold sighting in 1947 of a number of flying disc-shaped aircraft and, even more significantly, the incident during July the same year when an object is reported to have crashed in the New Mexico desert near Roswell, have become part of the iconography of contemporary UFOlogy. Less well-known are Devonshire reports from the same era which, although not quite as potentially climactic as the Roswell 'crash', are not without interest to the avid seeker after truth.

The first piece in the Devon puzzle comes from an item in the 'Round and About with Dennis H. Pratt' column in the *Exmouth Journal* of 9 December 1950. I make no apologies for quoting what may seem at first to be extraneous material, but I feel that it is important to see these events in as wide a cultural context as is possible. I should also explain the song referred to.

According to a colleague of mine, Andrew Dennis, the song ('Five little men in a flying saucer') has been featured by the BBC in their *Fun Songs Factory* and is a massive hit with the under-5s. It's a counting-down thing, like 'Ten green bottles', but starting off with five alien spacemen flying around the world in a flying saucer, looking at everything but liking nothing. This prompts one of them to fly away, leaving four. Finally there is just one little man left, who actually likes what he sees and stays.

Mr Pratt's 1950 column reads:

'If there were, as the song says, "two little men in the flying saucer", we saw [it] at Exmouth last Saturday afternoon… The "flying saucer" was seen by some of the Saturday afternoon gardeners on the Hamilton-Cranford allotments. Things are certainly pretty bad up there, thanks to the weather, but even such a mess need not have caused those "two little men" to scoot across the sky at such a furious rate. They could, at least, have had a look at the Brussels sprouts that were not all that bad. Down on the Maer the town reserves took a toss in the Geary Cup competition but the "two little men" were apparently not the least bit interested. They whizzed away towards Exeter – as we thought – as if old scratch was after them.

'It seems that the "two little men" had a look at the football matches in Somerset just about the same time, a little before four o'clock. Please let me make it clear that we didn't actually see the "two little men", they just came out of the song.

'Oh, but we did see the flying saucer and we have never before seen such a thing. It flipped across the sky just as other folk said these things do flip across the sky, and looked like a small watery moon, and left some sort of trail.

'Of course, we have never before seen a meteorite in daylight, but that is what we really and truly believe we saw on Saturday. We shall have to see something a lot more convincing to make us believe in flying saucers!'

I now move on a year. The next piece in the jigsaw, which has led some enthusisastic commentators to conclude that the British Government was actively involved in a minor-league UFO-related cover-up half a century ago, is also from the *Exmouth Journal* and is dated 13 October 1951.

'*Another Flying saucer?*
'A small number of people on Exmouth's sea front on Sunday evening at about 8.30 witnessed a curious phenomenon. What appeared at first to be a brilliant blue sky rocket travelled in a straight and horizontal course towards the North West and vanished in mid-air after a few seconds.

'The head was a cone of brilliant light blue and there was a comparatively short tail of golden light. The speed was much slower than that of the usual meteorite and there was nothing in the nature of a flash.

'The progress of the light was steady and the height did not appear to be great. The suggestion has been made that the apparition was a guided missile used in practise.'

A week later the front page carried the headline '*Flying Saucer was Guided Missile!*' and ran the following story:

'Reported exclusively in the *Exmouth Journal* last week, the "Flying Saucer" seen from Exmouth Sea Front on the night of October 7th proves to have been, as we suggested, a guided missile. It was, in fact, the biggest and fastest guided missile yet built by scientists in Britain, and it was on the secret list until late on Monday night.

'Two powerful motors drive the thirty foot rocket upwards at a speed of 2000 miles per hour. The missile is then guided along a radar beam to the target.

'A huge jet of flame is thrown out by the motor to launch the rocket and then boost it to high speed and when this fuel is spent the booster drops off. What was seen from Exmouth was undoubtedly the sight of the streamlined front half travelling under its own power'.

The story was complicated by another report the following year which, apparently at least, provides some vindication for this interpretation of events.

'*We saw Secret Weapon ten months ago*
'A number of Exmouth people are possibly amongst the first "civilians" to have seen Britain's answer to the Atom Bomber, a self-guided rocket in actual flight.

'Last Saturday Mr Duncan-Sandys, Supply Minister, revealed a fantastic new weapon, a guided rocket for use in defence against Atom Bomb air attack. Mr Sandys...saw trials at an experimental establishment at Aberporth, South Wales [this was presumably at the range now controlled by the Defence Evaluation and Research Agency (DERA), with target drones flying from Llanbedr, which has been conducting research since the mid 1950s] and afterwards because of military security he could not state precisely the actual performances, but the guided rocket can travel at well over two thousand miles per hour and reach heights greater than a bomber is likely to reach for years.'

I checked with an ex-BAe engineer and military historian who suspected that the figures given, ostensibly by Duncan-Sandys, were hyperbole to say the least. A thorough search has revealed that the missile referred to was probably an early version of the 'Blue Sky' or 'Fireflash' missile which, although an impressive weapon for the time, could not approach the figures claimed for it in the newspaper.

Missiles with that degree of performance were not tested for several years, and then only at the Woomera Testing Range in Australia. So what happened?

There is no evidence whatsoever that the British Government claimed the Exmouth sightings were of their guided missile. All the evidence I have points towards a journalist from the local paper putting two and two together and dreaming up a solution to fit in with his self-styled role as arbiter of truth and honesty in the New Elizabethan age. He also did his patriotic 'bit' to foil the menace of the Russian Bear by announcing an extraordinary weapon that didn't really exist. In short he probably made the whole thing up.

THE FIFTIES AND SIXTIES

The history of fortean investigation is full of tiny, and otherwise silly, coincidences which have, despite all the odds, turned into something far more significant. One day a friend and colleague of mine was having a cup of coffee in Exmouth when he was approached by a man who until a few months before had lived next door to him. He gave him a little booklet entitled *Flying Saucers over the West* by A B Bearne. It had been privately published in 1968 and his ex-neighbour had bought it for him as a present for the princely sum of 10p in a local charity shop.

Bearne's are a well-respected Devon firm of Auctioneers, so for a scion of this noble family to have lent his name to something gives west-of-England UFO research a level of *gravitas* which it would not otherwise have had.

Bearne's interest in the subject started with his own sighting in Torquay during the summer of 1950:

'I was mystified to observe a funnel-shaped stream of flames, chiefly white, descending, pointed-end first, in an absolutely silent and very peculiar manner – peculiar inasmuch that the point of the flames seemed to be "creeping" or "fingering" downwards.

'I stared most intently at this unusual and unaccountable sight, trying to think what it could possibly be, and was very mystified indeed. I at first wondered whether it could be a burning part of a plane which had caught fire and burst asunder at some high altitude, but this solution did not satisfy me because it was not falling straight down but coming at an unvarying angle and at a steady and apparently not very fast speed, and there was something peculiar about the forward point of the flames which at first I could not understand.

'After having been in my view for possibly about half a minute, the flames – or flaming object or objects – disappeared below the top of the roof of my house. Therefore, still very puzzled, I continued walking forward down towards the kitchen door at the side of my house, gazing straight ahead between my house and the next in the direction where I expected this strange object to appear on its downward path. In a very short while it again came into view, but now more strange still I observed not a long stream of flames but a roughly spherical "ball of fire", and instead of continuing in its former path downwards it was now travelling horizontally straight away in front of me in a southerly direction over Paignton towards Churston Ferrers and Higher Brixham, and at no very great height, possibly not more than 500 feet – but this was difficult for me to judge correctly, although a trained aircraft observer could probably have given an accurate estimate of the height.'

His report was far from being unique. Only four years later in 1954 two Torquay men reported seeing 'about 15 mysterious balls of fire in the sky' near the coast at Babbacombe. The two men were looking out to sea towards Weymouth. They later told newspaper reporters that 'they were an orange yellow colour like balls of fire, and as [we] watched [we] saw them go into a straight line and counted about 15 of them. They were moving quite slowly then, but they went into a cluster again and climbed very rapidly into the clouds and out of sight.'

One of the men later added: 'I never believed stories about flying saucers and such things before, but seeing is believing.'

The following account appeared in the Torquay *Herald Express* the next day:

'More witnesses came forward today to confirm reports, published in yesterday's *Herald Express*, that objects like fireballs had been seen from Torquay over the sea. Mr S J Hines, of Stover Golf Club, Newton Abbot, said he was on the Esplanade, Exmouth, on Friday afternoon when his son drew his attention to a number of round objects floating in the sky above the sea in the Weymouth direction. He added "They looked like balls of fire, just as they have been described in your newspaper." Mrs G H Bean of Paignton told the *Herald Express* that her mother and brother were both on Babbacombe beach at the same time on Monday as was mentioned in the first report. On returning home they had described what they had seen, and it was exactly as observed by the first two witnesses. Mrs Bean remarked that no one would ever believe their story as they, too, had always doubted the many reports of strange objects seen in the sky recently.

'Mr J J Sutton, also of Paignton, states that while watching from his bedroom window he saw the "fireballs" break one by one from the clouds and move slowly in a line over Thatcher Rock and then disappear towards Babbacombe.'

The *Exmouth Journal* has a number of historical reports. A strange object was seen in the night sky in October 1957:

'In an interview with the *Journal* Mr Bulling said: "I was coming out of my house about ten minutes past five on Tuesday morning and I looked across a clear blue sky to the west. I saw a light travelling at great speed. It was like a star but larger and at first I thought it was a jet plane, but it was travelling too fast for a jet. It was moving east towards the moon. As it appro-ached the moon it changed colour to orange and then I lost sight of it. I saw it for about 30 seconds."'

Police constable H L Sandercock walked out of Exmouth police station shortly after five the same morning and 'saw the object, like a large star racing towards the moon.' He lost sight of it after about a minute, he told a reporter at the time.

Unfortunately for UFO buffs, the date and the description provided give the secret of this particular sighting away. In October 1957 the Soviet Union stunned the world by launching *Sputnik 1*, the world's first artificial satellite. Although *Sputnik 1* was only about 0.6 metres in diameter, weighed 83 kilograms and could send only radio beeps towards the United States as it flew overhead around every ninety minutes, it had a profound effect on the world.

Shaken up by the persistent beep-beep-beep reminder of Russian skill in space, the US government began a crash programme to improve America's standing in science, technology, and engineering. Within a year after *Sputnik 1*, both NASA and ARPA (the Advanced Research Projects Agency) had been created. The National Defense Education Act provided loans to students and funding for educational programmes, especially ones in maths, science, and foreign languages. And in faraway Devonshire some elderly men continued to scan the skies after they thought they had seen a UFO.

Some sightings are, however, less easy to explain. Ten years later, on 28 April 1967, eight coastguardsmen, including Brian Jenkins, reported sighting through binoculars a cone-shaped UFO which they described as 'shining brilliantly'. Their description indicates that they believed it was made of metal. There appeared to be some sort of hatch on the underside. No one has been able to identify the craft.

THE SEVENTIES AND EIGHTIES

At the end of the 1970s there was another spate of sightings in East Devon. UFOlogist Nigel Wright remembers that in September 1977, together with a varying number of his friends, he often used to drive up to Woodbury Castle where the car park overlooks the Exe Estuary. They would take a picnic tea, and sit and watch in awe as nearly every night glowing balls of orange light – sometimes as many as four in an evening – would gently float inland from the Estuary, following the river towards Exeter in a rolling motion. They would get nearly as far upriver as the city and then disappear into a pinprick of light.

In 1978 as a police investigation into a local murder was at its height, coincidentally there was another spate of UFO activity in the area. The *Exmouth and East Devon Journal* for 28 October 1978 reads:

'Five young Lympstone girls talked excitedly this week about the UFO they claim to have seen hovering over Candy's Field on Monday night at about 7.00 and their statements were backed up by twelve year old Julie Hawkins, who said she saw the object from her bedroom, which overlooks the top of Meeting Lane.

'The five, Sharon Tooley, Clare Johnson, Angela Eyres, Tracey Bright and Glynis Uphill were sitting on top of a Wendy Hut in the field when they saw the object stop. "I was walking up the field with Tracey when we first saw it," said Glynis. "At first we thought it was a shooting star, but we could see a cigar shape. It was silvery-coloured, with lights.

'"When we got to the hut, we watched it for a while until it stopped over a tree. It was silent. We were scared, and we went into the hut and put a tyre against the door as a barricade. But we could see it through the cracks in the wall. It moved overhead and seemed to be starting to land. Then it went forward and sort of vanished."

'Paula Marker who did not see the object said that she reached the hut shortly afterwards and found the girls scared and screaming, and one of them was crying.'

There was a spate of UFO sightings almost a decade later in the summer of 1987. The first report of a particularly problematical object described as a 'Flying Fairground' was reported in the *Exmouth Herald* in August.

'A mystery object, described as "looking like a flying fairground", was spotted high in the night sky over Exmouth on Tuesday. Mr Gordon Baker spotted it travelling slowly in the sky. He had gone out into his garden, armed with a telescope in the hope of catching a glimpse of the planet Jupiter, which should have been visible in the clear sky. Instead, he said, he saw this object, which he sketched as it tracked over the town from the north-east to the south-west.

'After training a pair of binoculars on the two cross-shaped objects travelling close together, Mr Baker called his wife Gloria and asked a neighbour, Miss Heather Palmer, to look at the brightly-lit object. While watching it, the three saw an aircraft pass underneath much faster than the mystery object was travelling. Mr Baker said: "I believe the object was travelling at about 35,000 feet. Then I heard the noise of a jet aircraft. I saw it pass under the lit objects and I even checked with Exeter Airport to see if the pilot had reported seeing it. They said they had not received any reports. However, a man in air traffic control said he had had a couple of objects on his radar, but did not know what they were. We watched it for about 15 minutes until it disappeared on the horizon."

'"I don't know what it was but it certainly had hundreds of lights on it."

'Miss Palmer said: "Mr Baker knocked on my door and said "have a look at this." I went out on to the pavement and I could see these two lit-up crosses straight away with my naked eye.

'"He gave me a pair of binoculars to look at it, but I could see better with my own eyes. As I went out of the house, I looked at my watch and the time was eight minutes past ten. There was no noise at all. It was just moving slowly across the sky. Living here, you often see aircraft at night and they have flashing lights. These lights were all constant and white. I just don't know what it was."'

This report spawned a number of other reports of what appeared to be the same object that were published in the same newspaper a week later:

'Last week's UFO sighting over Exmouth has been confirmed by three more people. But the Ministry of Defence is not interested. A spokesman said this week: "If UFOs were hovering over one of our RAF bases, we would look into it. Otherwise the sightings are of no interest to us. In most of these reports, there is a logical explanation."

'He did not offer one for the object – described as "looking like a flying fairground" – seen over Exmouth on August 4th by at least six people, including Mr Tony Millington, a former RAF technician. Mr Millington and his wife Claire were leaving the Globe public house in the village when they saw brilliant lights towards Starcross. Mr Millington, who served in the RAF for 15 years, said: "It certainly was not an aircraft. When we got to the Green, we looked over the water towards Starcross and we saw these two large lights which were a sort of orange colour."

'"It is very difficult to say how high they were, but there was no noise at all. That is what seemed so odd to me. As we watched, the two objects seemed to get close together and I thought it was very, very odd. We watched the objects for about 15 minutes before they disappeared over the horizon towards Haldon Hill. The lights were uniform in brilliance."

'They were also seen by Mrs Elizabeth Tunmer from her mother-in-law's home in Granary Lane, Budleigh Salterton.

Mrs Tunmer sketched the object before returning to her home in Sussex. Her mother-in-law, Mrs Elizabeth Tunmer, said: "My daughter-in-law saw it quite clearly and watched it for several minutes.

'"To her, it appeared to be a lit-up object like an aircraft on its side. There was no noise but the lights on it were so strong and it was moving very slowly. She watched it until it was hidden from view by trees at the bottom of our garden. We just don't know what it was."

'Another witness was Mrs Pat Sampson of Withycombe Village Road, Exmouth, who thought at first the UFO was a Hercules plane refuelling from a tanker. But the curious thing was that there was no noise. "There were a lot of separate lights and one of the aircraft sent out an orange flare – which we have never seen before," she said. "Also, the Hercules is smaller than the tanker, but these two aircraft were the same size."'

A further note, the following week, sheds some light on this particular mystery:

> '102, Bradenham Beeches,
> Walters Ash,
> High Wycombe, Bucks.

'SIR – Recently, I received a copy of the *Exmouth Herald* of August 7th via my father who lives in Dawlish, in which you reported the appearance of a mysterious object in the night sky over Exmouth. From Mr Gordon Baker's graphic description of his sighting on August 4th I deduced that he had most likely observed a number of aircraft engaged in air-to-air refuelling.

'For this particular manoeuvre, the aircraft fly in close formation and at night the undersides of the tanker are illuminated with white floodlights to help the receiving aircraft to acquire visual contact. Enquiries at our main RAF tanker base revealed that a pair of VC10 tankers conducted a refuelling exercise over South West England on the night in question. Furthermore, one of the pilots was able to confirm that the aircraft flew over Exmouth in formation towards the South West at a height of 25,000 feet shortly after 10 p.m. He also recalled that both aircraft had the floodlights switched on.

'Air-to-air refuelling is carried out at a lower speed and engine power setting compared with airliners flying at similar heights. It is understandable, therefore, that the sound of the VC10s was inaudible to observers on the ground.

'The flight path of the tankers would not have been known to the authorities at Exeter Airport because aircraft flying high over Devon and Cornwall are controlled directly from the London Air Traffic Control Centre.

'I hope my explanation solves the mystery of the "flying fairground" to the satisfaction of Mr Baker and your other readers who shared his unusual experience.

MICHAEL WESTWOOD
Squadron Leader'

This effectively solves the puzzle. Or does it? It is a little odd that a former RAF technician was unable to identify such a common manoeuvre and it is also hard to reconcile the drawing by the original witness, Mr Baker, with the account given by Squadron Leader Westwood. It seems unlikely that a more bizarre explanation will be forthcoming. However, it should be noted that whilst the furore about the 'Flying Fairground' was at its height, Mr Baker, together with friends of his, witnessed several other objects which, if his sightings that were reported so widely in the local media are to be believed, bear no resemblance whatsoever either to aircraft of RAF Transport Command or to a 'Flying Fairground'.

'Thirteen mystery objects, all shaped like an inverted cup on a saucer, were seen above Exmouth at the weekend. The sightings were made and double-checked by a newly-formed network of UFO watchers based in and near the town. When one member of the group sees an object, he or she calls another keen amateur astronomer to check the sighting after giving the subject's description and course.

'Mr Gordon Baker of Blackmore Court, Exmouth, formed the network of sky watchers after people contacted him two weeks ago saying, like him, they had seen a mysterious "flying fairground" object over the town. On Friday night he spotted three saucer-like objects, another three on Saturday and seven on Sunday evening. He described each as being lit brightly when travelling at speed, but dim when they slowed down.

'He said: "These are a new lot of objects. They are not aircraft or comets, which can be easily recognised by their tails. They are shaped very much like a saucer with an inverted cup on them. When they go slow, their lights dim and then they change direction, before going off again at a terrific speed. As soon as I saw them I telephoned Bill O'Shaughnessey at Woodbury. He saw them and gave me a running commentary over the telephone. His wife was outside with a friend and kept relaying the information to him while I was on the phone.

'"Now we have a way of checking the direction in which these objects are travelling. I am making a record of the times and dates of all the sightings and who has seen them". Mrs Caroline O'Shaughnessey, of Woodbury Salterton, said: "I saw three objects travelling together and then split up and go different ways in the area of the Plough in the sky. They were certainly not something made on earth. They were too high and too bright."'

A few months later Mr Baker saw another object in the sky:

'Alien beings from outer space have apparently returned to take another look at Exmouth. Years after the last published reports of UFOs being sighted over the town, a flying saucer is claimed to have been spotted on Saturday evening. Mr Gordon Baker drew a rough sketch of the flying object which, he said,

21

was moving at a speed which he thought was around ten times the speed of a jet plane.

'He told the *Herald*: "I called my wife and neighbours who came out and saw it as well. The UFO had blue and white lights running around its rim. It was like neon signs flashing in a row of windows all around the edge."

'Mr Baker, an amateur astronomer, owns four powerful telescopes, one of them capable of magnifying sixty-fold, which he used at the time.

'He said: "The sky was completely clear of cloud at 8.30 on Saturday evening and there was almost a full moon when I went outside. I heard a sound in the sky, looked up and saw the lights of a Tristar airliner with three vapour trails behind it.

'"Through my telescope, I could see the plane's fuselage, although you wouldn't have been able to do so with the naked eye. Suddenly I saw a large circular object three times as big as an airliner towards the east. Blue and white lights were flashing around the edge of it. It was moving west. Then it stopped and hovered above the town for about three minutes. It headed north at great speed, stopped five miles away and hovered again.

'"That was when I called my wife and neighbours, thinking I might need witnesses who would say it really did happen. They didn't have to look through the telescope because they could see the circling blue and white lights quite clearly. After that, the UFO headed away to the west and hovered over the Exe Estuary before continuing to the west and vanishing."'

THE NINETIES

Many sightings in my records are of amorphous balls of light. The earliest of these is from 1987 when the *Exmouth Journal* printed an impressive picture of a glowing light surrounded by clouds and flying over the Exe Estuary:

'Exmouth amateur photographer Jim Brady is wondering if he inadvertently sighted [an] Unidentified Flying Object while taking a sunset shot over the Exe Estuary. For, after collecting his newly developed slides from the chemist, when Jim came to project the slide on the wall of his flat, there it was in all its glory – a shining white object in the western sky above Haldon Hills. "It's all a bit of a mystery how it got there. I've tried to rule out all the possibilities and I'm still baffled."

'It was about 4.30 p.m. on a winter's evening when Jim took the shot, so he ruled out the Evening Star. "There was no high flying aircraft around at the time and if the mark had been a spot of emulsion from the printer's it would have shown up more positively on the transparency", said Jim.

'"I suppose it could have been a Met Office balloon," he said, "but if it was it was a big one and why wasn't it there about fifteen seconds later when I took a second shot of the same sunset? It had just vanished."'

Three years later in 1990 there was another sighting:

'Three trainee teachers who spotted a mystery light over Exmouth at the weekend have asked if anyone can explain exactly what it was they saw. The three students at Rolle College reported the UFO sighting to Exmouth police but checks with the coastguard and other authorities have failed to come up with an answer. Coincidentally, police all over the Westcountry received numerous calls at the weekend after what is thought to have been a meteor was reported to have "scorched" across the night sky before coming down with a "bang" in Bridgwater Bay.

'The Exmouth students say the strange "moon-sized" orange ball of light was moving East to West and falling towards Lyme Bay off Exmouth – the wrong direction for the Bridgwater reports. First year B.Ed. students Lee Jones, from Weston-super-Mare, and Mark Marsden from Sussex, were watching a video with fellow third year American exchange student Stephanie Glover, in a ground floor flat at Kingsthorpe Hall of Residence, Rolle Road, at 9.45 p.m. on Sunday evening.

'They said their attention was attracted to the strange light in the dark night sky through the seaward-facing window of the flat.

'"We saw this light like an orange ball moving very slowly across the sky from our left to right. We saw it go down very, very slowly and then go out of sight below the trees on our horizon," said Mr Marsden.

'"It was like nothing we had ever seen before. We went down to the beach to see if something had come down in the sea but we could see nothing and two people we spoke to who were walking their dogs along the seafront said they had seen absolutely nothing," he added. The three have been the subject of some attention from fellow students since reporting the sighting and would now like to know if anyone else saw anything or can explain what the mystery light was.'

I tried to contact Mr Brady, but according to residents at Rivermead Court he had moved several years before and no one knew where he lived any more.

A year later, the *Exmouth Journal* printed a letter from Barbara Bellinger containing another sighting of an amorphous ball of light:

'"I visited Exmouth for three days last April and on the second night (April 3rd I think), in my hotel on the Beacon I couldn't sleep, and stood at the window – it was around 3.40 a.m and a still moonlit night – when suddenly an orange coloured "ball" rolled from one side of the bay (on the right) and disappeared at the other side. It was not so high as the stars (at least I don't think so) and was quite large. I could see the surface of it was not smooth but sort of roughed up. It was not shooting along but rolling over and over as a billiard ball does on a table.

"'I would be most interested to hear if anyone else has reported seeing it. It was a sort of "lit up" orange colour – not just orange if you know what I mean. I can tell you I did not sleep after that!'"

Nick Pope is a well-known character in British UFOlogy who has sometimes courted controversy. At one time he worked in Department AS2a of the Ministry of Defence where he was in charge of collating civilian UFO reports. In an interview with Michael Lindemann, a well-known American UFOlogist and broadcaster, he talked about another wave of West Country UFO activity:

'[There was] a wave of sightings that occurred on the 30th and 31st of March 1993. We had several hundred reports that came our way. Many of the witnesses were police. A lot of police in the southwest of the country, in Devon and Cornwall, saw something.

'Now, as with all of these big waves of sightings, a lot of the reports were fairly mundane, lights in the sky. But even so, it was quite late at night – most of these reports were between, say, 1.00 and 1.30 in the morning – and because there were police officers on night patrol, you're dealing with more than average recognition training, and people used to being out and about, and seeing lights and other things in the sky. Repeatedly, I heard the phrase, "This was like nothing I'd ever seen before in my life." People were genuinely spooked by this.

'What was generally reported were two lights, flying in a perfect formation, with a third, much fainter light. The lights were described as being in a triangle formation. It's quite possible they could have been three separate things flying in formation, but the impression from talking to witnesses was that this was a triangular craft with lights mounted on the underside, at the edges.

'I launched a full investigation. I made all the usual checks, trying to track down aircraft movement, satellite activity, airships, weather balloons, meteorites, etc, etc. I drew a blank – with one exception – and then put a report up the chain of command. The exception was a ballistic missile early warning sensor at RAF Fylingdales, in North Yorkshire. It is estimated that at some stage in the night there had been a rocket re-entry of, I think, Cosmos 2238, which might have caused a very brief firework display in the high atmosphere. It's just possible that some of the vague lights-in-the-sky sightings might have been explained in that way, although Fylingdales didn't seem very sure on whether [the satellite re-entry] was actually going to be visible from the UK at all.'

The next year, in 1994, another letter referring to a ball of light appeared in the *Exmouth Journal*:

'My husband and I were visiting Exmouth for a family wedding. On Sunday evening, March 22nd, we were driving towards Topsham at about 8 p.m with some friends, when, on the left, I saw a bright light in the sky. It was like a glowing fluorescent ball, not red but bright pink. It was not moving. It then appeared on the right side and much higher. After a few more seconds it just vanished.

'I have received two articles from your newspaper, one suggesting a distress flare – but I have never seen one move sideways across the sky – or a rabbit hunter's torch beam – I don't think so – cat's eyes, certainly not.

'Ever thought about UFOs?

'Mrs S E Smith'

The weirdest, and certainly the most spectacular, series of UFO sightings in Devon took place during the long hot summer of 1997. It started in early July when an Exeter man, who happens to be an acquaintance of mine, was looking east towards Exmouth, out of the window of his flat in Alphington Road. He saw a similar light. He remarked to researchers later that it seemed not to cast a light or a shadow but to be complete in itself. He watched it for a few minutes before it sped off at a great speed. A week later, on 25 July, two people were travelling east along the A30 at dusk when they noticed a cigar-shaped object in the sky over Woodbury Common. But it was two days later on Sunday 27th when things really began to get bizarre.

At lunchtime a Sea King helicopter was performing a mock air-sea rescue for the entertainment of the massed throngs of holidaymakers on Exmouth sea front. Among the enthralled audience was Dave Littlefield, an aviation expert and author, who was videotaping the exercise for his own archives.

Several days later, when watching the recording, a friend of his pointed out that behind the helicopter was a clearly visible silver light which appeared to be hanging motionless in the sky. The silver light was seen against the backdrop of a particularly distinctive bit of cloud, but when the helicopter returned to that section of the sky the light had vanished. They compared the light with the reflections from the shiny metallic parts of the helicopter. In appearance they were quite different, and computer enhancement suggests that the object was either circular or disc shaped, although it is impossible to tell whether it was in fact metallic or whether it was acting as its own light source.

That evening Channel Four showed a Roswell movie, together with a documentary containing the disputed Ray Santilli 'Alien Autopsy' video. Sceptics in the West Country media blamed the veritable outpouring of sightings which took place over the next few nights as being influenced by this televisual treat. The sheer volume of sightings, and the high degree of correlation between them, as well as the Exmouth video tape, make this hypothesis unlikely. I'll take at random a few of the sightings from that Sunday night – 27 July 1997.

William Fraser-Jennings, a telesales manager at Bushey Park, Budleigh Salterton, was with five friends on a hilltop near Budleigh Salterton, looking south to south-east. They noticed a bright white light which, because of the height of the hill, appeared at eye level, rose vertically, then blinked out about four minutes later. They watched it through binoculars and described the shape as being elongated horizontally, and later to the *Exmouth Journal* as being 'dish-shaped'.

Twenty minutes later they observed the same thing again for about four minutes. This time it moved northwards before disappearing.

At practically the same time (9.50 pm) a retired person in Torquay came out of a concert hall and saw a stationary bright yellowish 'thing' in the north east – the direction of Exmouth across the Exe estuary. He described it as being the size of a thumb held at arm's length and at an elevation of 20°. He only watched for a few minutes before it disappeared.

At about 10.00 in the evening, the mother of my best friend's girlfriend was looking out of the window of her house at Beer in East Devon when to the west she saw a bluish-white light zig-zagging across the sky. It appeared to be over Exmouth or Woodbury.

A few hours later, in the early hours of Monday morning, an Exmouth businessman saw a pair of bright blue lights over the sea zig-zagging around.

Then at between 4 and 5 in the morning, about three hours after the events recounted to me by the businessman, a couple were looking out of their bedroom window which faced west towards the Royal Marine camp at Woodbury. At an elevation of about 45° they saw a bright white light (of burning magnesium intensity) which moved up and down relative to the stars, but which looked smaller than the moon would have been. The wife told me they both felt scared because 'It felt close: I'd just never seen anything like it before'.

She telephoned my office on a number of occasions over the next few days. She seemed a likeable but very shy person who was more confused than anything else by her one and only excursion into what Dr Mike Dash, one of the guiding lights behind *Fortean Times* (a long-running journal of unexplained phenomena), described as 'The Borderlands'.

One of the most peculiar things about her experience is that her husband had a slightly different impression of the colour of the light they had seen, but other than that their reports coincided. The phenomenon of two witnesses of the same object describing different colours is well-known within UFOlogy and is, indeed, one I have encountered before.

The next night, 28 July, at 10.04 pm a young woman I shall call 'Tracey Wilson' was looking out of her bedroom window in a house on the eastern edge of Tiverton. Her father is a vehement non-smoker, but she was having a crafty cigarette and so was sure of the time of her experience. She saw an 'orange and white light' at an elevation of 30° moving northwards. The light was visible for about two minutes, then flared brightly before going out. Her main, indeed as far as I could gather, her only reason for not wanting her identity to be divulged was so that her father wouldn't find out she smoked cigarettes.

Forty-five minutes after Tracey was contravening her father's wishes, a retired police officer was halfway down his garden path in the Redhills district of Exeter, facing his house (to the south) and talking to his neighbour. The weather was clear, the temperature was in the mid 60s, it was dark and there was no visible moon.

He saw a bright white flash over the roof; his neighbour, nearer his own house, was facing north and didn't see it. Two minutes later there was a second flash to the right of the previous one, approximately south-west. And the third flash (this time also seen by the neighbour) was even brighter, in the west – towards Exmouth,

Each flash was half to three-quarters of a second in duration; bigger (and brighter) than Venus; separated by about two minutes; and at an elevation of approximately 75-80°.

On the evening of Tuesday 29 July, Barry Payne, a plumber from Dawlish, was looking eastwards over the sea. He saw a bright orange and white light heading from south to north towards Exmouth. The flight was interspersed with zig-zag movements. Mr Payne is familiar with aircraft movements and is convinced that this was different. He watched it for about five minutes before it disappeared.

Just before midnight on Friday 1 August someone identifying himself as 'Shane' telephoned me from an Exmouth phone box to explain that he had seen two bright lights zig-zagging around, up on Woodbury Beacon. A few hours later, David Nelson was near Exeter Airport. He was looking north-east towards Exeter and saw an object at an elevation of 45°. It was corkscrewing (i.e. moving left, right, up and down) and getting brighter; then it died out. Its colour was initially white, and it changed to yellow.

At about the same time an elderly Exmouth lady saw a strange whitish object to the south-east. It was triangular, and 'misty round the edges. It didn't move, and it didn't twinkle.' She watched it for about three minutes.

On 6 August between 11.30 pm and midnight, five members of the Sanders family were having a barbecue in their back garden of Willacombe, an estate in Tiverton, when the telephone rang. It was a neighbour who told them to look up quickly at the night sky. They saw two white lights horizontal to the horizon; one larger than the other, and with the smaller one 'chasing' the larger one east in the direction of Cullompton. They were both circular in shape.

At 21.30 on 11 August 'Anna Epson' (a pseudonym, although

I have her real name and telephone number on file) was driving along the South Zeal to Throwleigh road on the edges of Dartmoor, with her sister who was on holiday from London. They both saw a star-like whitish light moving steadily across the north of the sky in an easterly direction towards Lyme Bay. She told me, 'If it hadn't been moving, I'd have thought it was just an average star'. It was at an elevation of approximately 45°. They watched it through binoculars for several minutes and noted that there didn't seem to be any change in the diameter of the object. They did note, however, that it moved in a zig-zag motion, which implied that, whatever they were looking at, it wasn't a satellite.

One might well ask why so many local witnesses contacted me rather than the local police or the South West Witness Support Group. I should point out that several local newspapers had run pieces on the sightings, and had quoted my telephone number as a contact point. At my request the specific details of what had been seen were kept to a minimum so that I could retain as much scientific objectivity as possible!

Half an hour after my own sighting (see the introduction on page 3) on 12 August 1997, two young men walking on Exmouth sea front saw two red lights behaving erratically. I met one of them at the BUFORA (British UFO Research Organisation) conference at Sheffield and he told me they were 'whizzing along just above sea level.' His friend, who works for British Aerospace, saw them in greater detail, but preferred not to talk to researchers, even in confidence, because he is involved with government defence work.

'Mark' (of Cowley Bridge, Exeter) works for British Rail and was on duty on the night of the 12th/13th. He was somewhere in the Exeter area on a train. At about 2.15 am he saw two balls of white light (with corona haze possibly due to fog) at an indeterminate distance with an elevation higher than 45° coming from east Devon towards Exeter. They were flying fairly fast –

faster than aircraft using Exeter airport. The one in front was going slower than the following one, which was zig-zagging. The balls of light 'appeared to be the size of an old half-pence piece'.

Two days later Exmouth witnessed a night of high strangeness unprecedented in its history! At 9.00 pm, Alan Gibbons was with friends in his garden facing north, and saw a very large stationary flashing light at 60°.

Half an hour later, two delivery people saw what was apparently the same object flying from north to south at an elevation of between 70° and 90°. They described it as a 'white, star-like object heading north'.

Over the next seventy-five minutes six members of one family living on the Littleham Estate, Exmouth, all experienced different UFO phenomena. The following report is taken directly from Nigel Wright's log of the evening's activities:

'21:30 Mother saw bluey star-like object heading E to NE 45°; disappeared suddenly; reappeared and there were two; changed direction & headed N.

'22:10 Took 16 yr old son out; both saw one object. They described it as "a steady bluish-white light travelling slowly over the Estate at a fairly low altitude". It was reportedly coming in from the sea at Lyme Bay towards Woodbury Common.

'22:30 Entire family (6) saw same object but heading from N back to E.

'23:15 Youngest son (15) with binocs saw expanding & contracting light 40° in N, green/red flashing lights on trailing edge of a "left-handed crescent shape".'

This last sighting was corroborated by an elderly lady from East Budleigh who reported looking out of her bedroom window when she saw what she described as a 'bright, elongated cigar-shaped craft with wing-like projections' hanging vertically in the sky above her. She said that it then changed shape as if it had rotated and headed out to sea over Lyme Bay.

A few days later she wrote a detailed letter to my colleague Nigel, including a rough sketch of the object, in which she described her sighting in more detail and also told of another sighting, albeit a vague one, from earlier in the evening:

'I wonder if the "wings" are something being given off from the main object – but they have a shape. It is definitely something unusual. They look delicate like gold tracery.

'I have also seen something flashing red when I went out at about 10 p.m. that moved quite quickly before it disappeared from my view, but was not like a shooting star.'

By the time Nigel had been informed of these events other reports were flooding in from all over the town. An elderly couple rang in from a phone box on the Estuary itself. They had seen an orange bright light 'low in the sky' travelling slowly from the estuary towards Haldon.

An anonymous Royal Marine (age 20) also phoned in and reported a stationary orange object with green lights to each side which appeared to move backwards and forwards, and then disappeared. He was facing east, and the object was at an elevation of approximately 45°.

Either Nigel or Sue, his wife, were on the telephone to me every half an hour, keeping me abreast of developments. The following night Nigel, who had been with the rest of the ESP group when we experienced our sighting on the 12th, saw a steady bluish-white light about the magnitude of Venus but with a distinctly circular shape. It moved from the west to the south-east at a slow to medium pace (the same sort of speed as a propellor-driven aircraft), before turning north and fading away. It was below the low cloud deck at an elevation of between 30° and 40°.

However, they weren't the only witnesses of a strange object that evening. The elderly lady from East Budleigh rang Nigel excitedly to say that the same object had reappeared for a second night and that she had watched it for about twenty minutes. She had even managed to take a photograph of the mysterious 'craft' – for this is what she was convinced it was. But much to our collective disappointment (although not greatly to our surprise), when the film was developed the whole thing – rather than merely the frames she had attempted to take of the UFO – were blank.

This is a syndrome which occurs over and over again in the annals of forteana and it is one that is most frustrating to the investigator. All too often a potentially valuable piece of film doesn't come out, is over exposed, is double exposed, is stolen, or is lost.

On two consecutive nights over the weekend of 16/17 August Diane, from Colebrooke near Crediton, was taking her dog along the Tumulus walk (between Spreyton and Colebrooke) at 10 pm. On both evenings she saw a very bright star-like blue-white object in the north-west at an elevation of about 45°. She told me how she had watched it for around twenty minutes on each occasion: whereas on the Saturday it had just hovered in the sky before 'blinking out of existence', on the Sunday she saw what appeared to be the same light zig-zagging erratically across the sky.

One day in late August a group of us, including Nigel Wright, Graham Inglis and myself, decided that enough was enough and that we really should try to collate the enormous amount of information we had gathered. We spent a laborious afternoon trying to do so. Even as we typed and telephoned witnesses to confirm the salient points of their experiences, more reports were coming in. That afternoon alone we had five telephone calls from eye witnesses. The situation was rapidly getting out of hand.

Mrs Turner, an elderly lady from Topsham, saw glowing balls of light nearly every night for over a week. They always appeared between 10.15 and 11.45 pm, and she described them as 'bright star-like objects with a pillar on top and a smaller star-like object on top of that' – a description somewhat reminiscent of that from the witness from East Budleigh who had seen, and attempted to photograph, an object in the sky a few days before.

Mrs Turner said that they 'wobbled as they moved' and furthermore she was convinced they were trying to contact her. She was not alone in her supposition. When Nigel's wife (who was, initially at least, a complete sceptic about all matters even slightly fortean) had her own sighting towards the end of August, she insisted to Nigel: 'That thing's watching us!'

Then, in the middle of September 1997, the sightings finished as suddenly as they had begun, and we, at the Exeter Strange Phenomena Research Group HQ, were left to puzzle over the data we had collected and to try and make some sort of sense of it all.

FURTHER UFO MYSTERIES

The sightings of mysterious big cats on the moorlands of the West Country are well known. Most people, myself included, believe they are the descendants of animals released into the wild in the wake of the 1976 Dangerous Wild Animals Act. Tavistock-based UFO researcher, Joan Amos, believes differently however.

'For some time,' Joan told me, 'I've had good reason for thinking there is a connection between big cats and UFO sightings. The first case which I had investigated personally that led me to these conclusions was in March 1982 when a CB radio user was on Dartmoor one night, talking to a lady in Cornwall. Seeing a light behind him and thinking it was a car, he turned – and what he saw frightened him so much that he ran back to his vehicle.

'About forty feet [12 metres] in the air was a flying object shaped like an egg with the bottom cut off, shining a huge beam of light onto a pony which was rearing up and whinnying with fright. The bell-shaped craft appeared to have a fin on one side and underneath was a ring of small lights that seemed to be turning around. The craft was completely silent.'

Within days of this incident, a strange cat turned up at a farm about a mile away. According to the farmer, Mr Knowles, it was a very weird animal which also had an odd effect on the farm dog, which was a faithful sheepdog that went everywhere with its master. On this occasion it hid under the table and refused to come out. It was the first time it had ever behaved like this.

The farmer showed Joan where the beast had leapt over a wall. He described it as having 'a snout like a pig, wet and quivering, and moving from side to side'. When his powerful torch had shone into its eyes, there was no reflection at all. The head was like a colt's and the face was long, with pointed ears turning forward. It had a large body, with a drooping stomach, and a tail like that of a greyhound curved between its legs.

This report intrigued Joan, and she decided to hunt through back copies of *Flying Saucer Review* for similar cases. In volume 26 #1 Charles Bowen wrote an article hypothesising that mystery animals were involved closely with UFOs. He described how an alsation dog cringed frightened in a corner when a 'puma' with a foul smell made nocturnal visits to the farm where he lived. These visits were usually preceded by strange lights, from an undefinable source, playing on the roofs of the farm buildings. He stated: 'We should be prepared to accept that UFOs and alien animals are inextricably linked.'

In volume 15 #5 there is a description of an animal not dissimilar to the one seen by Mr Knowles, the Dartmoor farmer: 'It had a brown head, large black eyes, and a nose extraordinarily like that of a pug. Its left ear was pricked, but the other one hung down like it was torn.'

As well as searching through her archives, Joan Amos began collecting contemporary reports of big cats and UFOs. She concluded that the South West seems to be especially prolific for sightings of both. Reports of animals point towards black leopards, pumas – and even a family of lynx. After asking around, she found that her hairdresser had seen a large cat on Dartmoor and that her travelling fishmonger had a customer who regularly placed an order for fish which he fed to lynxes that often came into his garden.

In September 1993, just before 'the beast of Bodmin' became a local household phrase, Joan received a spate of UFO reports. Huge silent craft and balls of light were seen at low altitudes around Dartmoor. She also told me about a report from a man who had walked the moor for thirty years and who had witnessed an area of 'disturbance':

'Large granite boulders were uprooted and some have disappeared altogether. This was in an inaccessible location with no signs of wheel marks or footprints. The disturbed area was almost circular, approximately 48 metres wide from north to south, and 35 metres wide from east to west. There was a dip in the centre of the circle three to four feet [a metre or so] in depth. The grass was visibly flattened, and boulders weighing more than half a ton had been moved four or five feet [1.2–1.5 metres] – the impressions of [where they had previously been] were still visible. Turfs had been ripped up.'

Parts of the moors are used by the armed forces for various exercises, and some people have suggested that the test of a secret weapon is responsible for these otherwise unexplained events. This is perhaps not so far fetched. Until it became a matter of public record in 1998, who would have believed that this part of the country had been used in the 1960s for germ warfare tests, with the release of bacteria by the military?

The 'animals and UFOs' theme is widespread, with many cases on file in which animals have reportedly been seen on spacecraft. The fictional Wellsian concept of alien races studying humanity's activities is a familiar one in science fiction, but Joan Amos concludes that, for some yet to be determined reason, it's our animals that are currently being scrutinised.

Tales of animal teleportation are not uncommon either. Joan heard of a cow which was apparently teleported from one field to another, and there were burn marks on its sides. She tried to get more details on this case, but the farmer refused to discuss the matter. One possible non-UFO explanation is that it was a failed cattle-rustling attempt. However, this doesn't get away from the fact that reports of UFO encounters do often involve sightings of animals.

CONCLUSIONS

Many people still believe that Unidentified Flying Objects are indeed alien spacecraft. This is called the Extra Terrestrial Hypothesis (ETH). However, many researchers, including me, feel this explanation is unlikely. Although the universe is infinitely big, and the existence of extraterrestrial intelligences is almost a statistical certainty, its sheer size combined with the impossibility (under the laws of conventional physics) of faster-than-light travel makes it seem severely unlikely that the UFOs reported all over the world almost daily can actually be alien spacecraft.

Another large group of people believe that the objects seen in the skies of the world are in fact terrestrial in origin, and that they are part of secret military technology belonging to the British, American or Russian governments. Whilst it is certain that at any given time all the world's major military and industrial powers have secret technology at least fifteen years ahead of anything that can be seen at the Farnborough Air Show, it is equally certain that they do not test this technology in broad daylight over the rolling hills of the Devon countryside.

So, although it seems undeniable that some of the objects seen are indeed terrestrial hardware, and whilst it would be foolhardy to dismiss totally the possibility that a very small number of UFOs are alien spacecraft, it seems we have to search elsewhere for a convincing explanation.

In this book I have suggested that a number of incidents, such as the 1957 object (which turned out to be *Sputnik*) and the 'flying fairground' (which was probably two RAF planes refuelling in mid flight) had a perfectly rational explanation. It's likely that some of the other sightings are equally easy to explain.

A number of the 1997 incidents, for example, were probably communications satellites and others were misidentifications of planets. However, a large portion of the incidents reported are not easy to explain at all.

We have to look at the phenomenon of UFOs in more of a metaphysical light. As F Halliday pointed out in his classic book *The Dragon and the Disc*, there is a burgeoning body of evidence to link some UFO incidents with other types of apparently disparate paranormal activity. During my researches I managed to draw distinct parallels between the 1997 UFO wave and a string of other strange occurrences happening at the same time in the same place, and *often* to the same people.

There seems to be a definite link between the sightings of UFOs and the appearances of strange animals and crop circles, and what are commonly known as alien abductions, as well as other more sinister phenomena.

I believe that somehow these are all manifestations of the collective subconscious of our society. In some way we don't yet understand we manage to manifest our deepest cultural fears into a semi-tangible form. In 1909, when the two girls saw a 'mystery airship' hovering over Exmouth seafront, it was a manifestation of the national trepidation about the forthcoming war with Germany. In the years immediately following World War II, when the whole earth had been terrified by the events of Hiroshima and Nagasaki, the technological hopes and fears of the western world were mirrored by pan-global sightings of items of strange technology that dwarfed anything terrestrial governments were able to manufacture. Finally, as we face up to the challenges of a whole new millennium, we are confronted by manifestations of strange alien races beyond our comprehension.

Whether I am right or whether I am wrong, the phenomena (whatever they are) continue, and I am reminded of the words of an ancient Chinese philosopher who once stated that 'the more we see, the less we know'.

I think that sums it all up really!